HARUKO AND I

ALBERT VICENT

Order this book online at www.trafford.com
or email orders@trafford.com

Most Trafford titles are also available at major online book retailers.

Print information available on the last page.

ISBN: 978-1-4907-8169-3 (sc)
ISBN: 978-1-4907-8170-9 (e)

Trafford rev. 04/12/2017

 www.trafford.com
North America & international
toll-free: 1 888 232 4444 (USA & Canada)
fax: 812 355 4082

Always

With forever
Now, and in the ever
Now, and – with always
In the future
That's where we'll go
That's with the lovely
And with love
Together we,
Will fly
With the Eternal
With forever.

About Haruko and I

Her name was Haruko, she was from Japan. We were married when I was in the Army in Yokohama Japan at the American Consulate office November 30ᵗʰ 1951. This is a story she told me of her early childhood years. When she was only about 12 years old, she told me a little stream that was only about two feet deep, being a child she planned to jump over it. She had a baby strapped on her back, and didn't make it across. Was carried quite some distance down the stream by the rapidly moving current of the stream. Then caught an overhanging branch and proceeded to pull, herself and the infant strapped to her back from the stream. She had been on her way to school, Haruko's mother had hired her out to work, clean house, and babysit for another family to provide funds for the family. This was a practice done years ago by some families in her country at the time.

The child had to work for the family and was hired for many years to pay back funds paid for this agreement between the families. The child could go to school sometimes. Education at that time was not a big deal to some families especially to Haruko's mother because her mother had little education. When Haruko with a baby strapped to her back fell into the little creek, she was on her way to school. After falling in the creek and getting out, she had to go back to the house where she worked, then change clothes. At the house she was reprimanded for jumping the stream with the baby on her back by the child's mother she worked for. The reprimand must have been quite severe, because Haruko was over 80 years old when telling this story to me and it happened when she was 12 years old. It made a lasting, impression on her mind.

When she went to school she always had to take the baby because her mother had made that type of arrangement with the family for a certain amount of money. Haruko said she had to work several years to pay off the agreement made by her mother to the family. She said on weekends sometimes she could go home to be with her family, but when she could go to school she had to take the baby and when the baby cried she had to always leave the classroom because it was a distraction. She said some of the other children babysit at school also, but not many. This was a common practice in her country years ago, but not now. Haruko was born in 1921 and it's 2016 now, much has changed since then. Years later when Haruko arrived at her teenage time of life, her mother committed her to work as a waitress in a whiskey bar which didn't last long. Because of the war in her country, with Japan and America.

When World War 2 started, Haruko was residing at the place of her birth Yamanashi-ken Japan war reached there too. She said she witnessed some bombing and strafing from war planes. She continued to work selling drinks, people still consumed alcohol. Her mother was then working in Yokohama and her new stepfather wanted her to come live in Yokohama. Once there she liked the area and told her relatives in Yamanashi-ken she would be staying in Yokohama. There she got a job operating a lathe making the lead bullet part of ammunition, the pointed part of a bullet.

Of course the war was carried on in a much larger scale in Yokohama than in Yamanashi-Ken because Yokohama was an industrial city and Yamanashi-Ken was in the country. A lot of large bomber planes like B-29's would come Haruko said, in great numbers. Dropping bombs and fighter planes like P51's would strafe with their machine guns, shooting anything in sight. She said the women and others were taught to beat the

2

enemy with sticks if possible. One time, she said a man parachuting from his stricken aircraft was beaten with sticks by the people on the ground. They later found out he was a Japanese serviceman and he later died. Haruko said she did not participate in that incident. She was told about it by others.

During the war, safe places were made for civilians in the mountainsides. During large air raids women, children, and the elderly were allowed to enter first. She remembered one time when they went in for about one and a half or two hours of intense bombing attacks before they were allowed to leave the shelter. She recalled that during this particular incident, when they were allowed out, Yokohama was red with a blazing fire everywhere. The whole city was on fire. They checked their homes and many were destroyed with water gushing from broken pipes. Wars terrible, but it seems at times it is part of life.

Haruko had much wartime experience. Not by choice, but she was where and when the war happened. After the war, things changed. While Haruko's life was progressing in Japan another person she would later meet eight years later who was her junior in years, was growing up in America. Attending kindergarten, elementary school, and doing things children do. He was finishing elementary school, reading books and becoming very fond of the countries of Japan and China, and reading much about them. After elementary school this person, who was myself, entered and finished four years of high school. I was then 17 years of age. The 17 years were very interesting too, having done the many things children do and having grown in a wee little town in Michigan call Peacock. The town had only about 35 or 40 people at that time with no sewage, or electricity… strictly country, which was good in a way because I got to see so much wildlife. There were lots of little gardens and much, little farm life. I attended an agricultural high school. I never wanted to become a farmer, but found the agricultural studies interesting.

During the teenage years I acquired automobiles and became interested in them. I became quite a mechanic removing engines and overhauling them, transmissions, installing clutches, most vehicles then were stick shift type. I did pretty much everything on vehicles and enjoyed it. I followed this type of work in the military later, it may have helped in some way. I'll never know, but that was the type of work I did in the military during the time I met Haruko and we later married. Anyway, my type of work was needed in the area I was sent, where she was. We met and the rest is history, Vicent history through the years.

The last year of high school in the month of March an Army Recruiting Sergeant came to our high school in March of 1947 and took names of those that might be interested in the Army. I gave him my name and forgot about it he didn't though. In the month of May this recruiting sergeant came to my house, my brother and I were sitting on the porch. The sergeant said "Hi Albert, are you ready to go?" I said, "Go where?"

He said, "Go in the army."

At that I became interested, because I was out of school and there was nothing to do. No one talked about college much back then. Like now it's expected for students to go on to college or some type of further training after high school. Not too many even got through high school in my little town of Peacock. So when the recruiting sergeant said are you ready to go and I said where, I was quite interested because I didn't know what I could do in Peacock, at that time. We were cutting trees with a crosscut saw with one man on each side of the saw, we pulled the saw back and forth to cut down a tree. Cut it into 8 foot lengths, and was paid $0.25 for each 8foot length. They were later taken to a sawmill and made into railroad cross ties. It was very hard work. There was also a small-town, Baldwin Michigan about 12 miles away where my brother and I could sometimes get work when a storekeeper there had a 50 Tonrail road flatcar of coal. We could unload the car with shovels and deliver it on trucks to homes. That was untimely work and very hard, and very dirty.

Me

I want to see me
Where is me
What happened to me
Where can I aim
To be the same
As before
I want more of me
I seem to have lost me
I want to see me
Where is me
What happened,
To me.

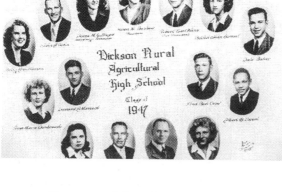

So when the sergeant said "I can give you the test right now Albert." I was really interested, after browsing in my mind of my future in Peacock. I said "yes." and the sergeant went to his car to get the test. I completed it in about 10 minutes. He quickly checked it and said that I passed the test. He also said if I passed the physical that I was in the Army. "I'll be back in 2 weeks to pick you up. Get everything done that you need to do."

"Okay" I told him. "I have to put the engine back in my mother's old model A Ford truck over there."

In 2 weeks he returned and I was ready to go. I took my physical and passed it and was sworn into the army in Dearborn Michigan on May 27th 1947. Having finished high school, I think maybe May 15th or 17th of 1947. I then went to Fort Monmoth New Jersey and took basic training there. Then went to Camp Lee Virginia where I took a wheel vehicle mechanic course and came home on furlough for about 2 weeks. The Army then sent me to Camp Stoneman California and then by troop ship on the E.D. Patrick to Yokohama Japan. It took about 2 weeks by ship. The Pacific Ocean gets quite rough in the month of January. I traveled in January of 1948. When I got to Japan I remember standing on the deck on the front part of the ship looking out at several little boats putt, putt, putting around in front of our ship with men wearing shoes that look like gloves on their feet. Of course there were called Ta-Bi footwear, quite common in Japan and have been used for years in that country.

I saw a small coca cola sign on a little shop and thought what kind of country is this? The sign looked quite old and weather-beaten, like it might have been there for years. A lot started spinning and occurring in my mind after seeing the American sign mixed with all

4

the other Japanese signs in Japanese writing. It created a feeling of curiosity, adventure, light reflection, and why, all at the same time a feeling that was different, also welcoming. The ship continued to move slowly until we docked at Yokohama Harbor where we walked down the gangplank with all our gear and off the ship. Was later sent to Camp Zama where we stayed for about 2 weeks. I was then sent to a camp in Yokohama called the 76 AAA (Anti-

Aircraft Artillery) located near Idogaya in Yokohama. I remember the streetcar number 10 would always stop near the camps front gate at a stop called Idogaya. I think that was the name of the stop. Anyway, I remember the number 10 Street car came by there.

After I met Haruko, lots of times she and I would catch the streetcar and ride down past Bon-Do-Bashi streetcar stop and walk down the main street of Yokohama. I think that was about 62 years ago now, and much water has passed under the bridge since that time. But we would walk down to a little place across the street from a big PX (post exchange) where they had a little donut shop that sold doughnuts & Fried Chicken. At the time that was the only place in that area that type of food was available in 1948, and Haruko liked donuts and fried chicken. We would then walk around Yokohama, which was a nice place to spend the afternoon when I was off duty.

Past the PX and donut shop across a little bridge, I remember there was a hospital for GI's called the 55th station Hospital. I remember taking Haruko there for some kind of test when we were fixing our marriage papers or getting ready to go to America after finishing my tour of duty in Korea in 1952. Kind of got off track a bit a few paragraphs back I was writing about being 18 years of age and just arriving in Japan on a troop ship at Yokohama Harbor and going to Camp Zama from there being assigned to the 76 AAA (Anti-Aircraft Artillery) unit in Yokohama where a streetcar number 10 stopped at a place called Idogaya near our camp. That has been some time ago. I'll be 87 years of age this August 2016 if all is ok between the Creator and I. I was 18 years old at the time I was sent to that unit.

The unit played a part in this story too because having been assigned to it that part of my life's plan was where I met Haruko. We then unknown to each other began this lengthy life journey of Haruko and I of which I now write. It's all part of a large plan which has flowed through the years with children, grandchildren, great grandchildren, great, great grandchildren, in-laws, numerous friends, and a great life.

Back to the 76 AAA in Japan, it was a good unit. I was assigned to C battery. Stayed there a few months,it was a half-track unit, the whole 76 unit was. I was a mechanic there, later was transferred to headquarters battery. They wanted me over there and I liked it there, I remember the first sergeant. His name was first sergeant Johnson, everyone called him Rick he was a good first sergeant and I liked him, the 76 was a good outfit.

After I was in Japan for a short while, I met this young lady and her name was Haruko. She was older than I, by about 8 years, but we got along good, really good. She took me to meet her family. Her family and I got along good they were always nice, very nice to me.

Picture

A picture you gave me (of you)
When first we met
And will have it with me
All my days.
It was with me all the
58 years of our marriage
For all to see
When you were called
By the Creator.
Is with me now on the wall
It stays, I see it
When I exercise each morning
Of every day
The picture (of you) you gave me
When first, we met.

———⟨◈⟩———

That was in the year of 1948 even now many years later. They are still very nice to me when I go to Japan to visit. They are like family of course, they are family. Because Haruko and I were married for 58 and a half years until the Creator called for her, I really miss her. She was a wonderful woman and a most wonderful wife.

When I got to Japan in 1948, there were not many cars. What few there were, many ran on charcoal for fuel. Little fires in a stove type fixture held the fire at the rear of the vehicle, a large pipe on top of the vehicle, carried fuel from the fire to the engine where it was processed by engine mechanisms to combustible material to run the engine. Sometimes the buses would stop on inclines, the driver would set the handbrake, go to the rear of the bus, put a block under the wheel and crank up the fire a bit, then remove the wheel block disengage the handbrake and away we would go again. The passengers all knew what the driver was doing. I thought maybe I did too, it was interesting though. Haruko and I rode the buses sometimes the streetcars they were more fun, at least to me they were… those old street cars. The driver appeared to drive standing, but he may have had some kind of stool. I remember the driver always standing though, ringing a bell to start after picking up a passenger. He would step on a little whistle that made a noise and pull on a lever type handle. The farther back he pulled the handle it seemed the faster the streetcar went. In a way the streetcar would go swinging down the streetcar track, swaying left and right it was fun. Quite like the Toonerville Trolley in the comic strip of the American newspapers of that time in the 1940's. Excuse me, I got off subject. I was writing about the charcoal burning vehicles. They were interesting, for I had never seen anything like that before, and had only read about vehicles powered by charcoal during the war. We had gasoline rationing during the war, but no charcoal burning vehicles.

I was enjoying my tour of duty in Japan, and the months moved fast. Only being 17 years of age when enlisting in the Army, for 3 years, the months were passing quickly. I was not thinking of reenlisting or anything like that at that time, and time passed rapidly. I put had in nearly eight months before leaving America. Having basic training, army school training, and travel time across the United States to various places, time had gone fast. Three years went pretty quickly. If one does speak of reenlisting where they are overseas or wherever, especially overseas and in Japan like I was at that time, a few months prior to discharge time, the serviceman was usually sent back to the states.

Being young, I didn't think about things like that my time passed rapidly. I only stayed maybe for 15 or 18 months in Japan. I was really enjoying everything. The duty was nice, the country was nice, Haruko and her family were nice, then abruptly it all finished. It just finished, I was on a troopship going back to America and soon after about 2 week's ship travel across the ocean, I was back in America. On my return trip to America, my legs swelled, got quite large on the ship and I had to go to the hospital when I got off the ship. I was sent to Madigan General Hospital in Tacoma Washington where I stayed for about 6 months. I was later told I had nephritis and they did not think I would make it. I was not aware of that though, so the Creator helped me a lot. Together we made it through. When I got out of the hospital my 3 year's enlistment was nearly finished. I had to do something pretty quick, because military life had kind of gotten to me and I certainly did not want to go back to the little town of Peacock Michigan where I grew up. There was no work nothing to do there, except to cut timber drive coal carrying trucks, do farm work.

Love

What is love, what is love
I ask you, what is love
Oh it comes, from God above
But what is love, what is love.

Oh to me, love is free
Comes from God, down to me
But to you, is love free
What is love, please tell me.

In this world, love seems far
Love seems far, on a star
But God love's, you and me
And love's there, and it's free

If you love, and it's true
You love God, God loves you
We know God, he is true
Love is there, love for you.

Chorus
Oh, love is Faith and love is Hope
Love is trust and love is care
And it comes from God above
When God sends Eternal love.

All that was real hard work, and all without the future I wanted. So I reenlisted in the military for 6 years this time and it seemed like a good thing to do and for me it was, life's been good. The Creator has been good and I can't complain. Whatever it is, this togetherness, this happens between people, care, love, whatever it may be called, it's there it's, silent. It speaks to each person, seems like differently because all the time after Haruko and I met. I know my military duty was one thing, I always tried to do my best to do my duty as a service man and I always still do, always will. With Haruko this togetherness, this care, love for each other was there, always there, reaching silently through darkness, sunlight, moon, and twilight, reaching, reaching, touching with feeling. It seems all through our 58 and a half years of togetherness and also through the years from when first we met in 1948, because we married in 1951.

I must go back. It seems like I'm going back quite a lot in the writing of this book, I guess because Haruko has been called, was called by the Creator in April 2010, April 15th 2010. I'm writing from memory of our years together, which comes randomly. So sometimes I must go back, kind of put things together. Don't get me wrong, all the years were great, my military life I spoke of that before. I always tried my very best to do my very best as a military serviceman, also my best as family man, and I hope I did. Haruko I know and always will feel she was a wonderful person, a wonderful wife. Through our many years together down to the very last minute were the very best, of course we had our little disagreements. I'm sure every family has, but we most always tried to settle them somehow before sundown, because for some reason small things seem to sometime grow overnight, then they are worse the next day. So we would always try to stop them as soon as possible and the years flowed by that way, 58 and a half years. The Creator was good to us, really good, thank you Creator.

I always will think the Creator had a lot to do with our meeting, because I was way over in Peacock Michigan and she was way over in Japan. Thousands of miles away, apart and we met, the Creator must have arranged it.

Doves

Two doves just landed
Here together they flew
As they came by
And together they stay
They must know
Each other
At least it seems so
Today
Two doves
The two doves
That flew here.
So quiet
As they came today
It seems…
Doves speak- Doves way- silently.

Memory

I looked and looked
And looked for you
Then I remembered
You're always
In my memories
That's a wonderful
Most beautiful place
To remember and be
Staying
There…
There in memory
Stored in memory, my memory
I found you lovely as always
In memory.

I always think so anyway. Feels good to think that way. We both, family too felt, that way we raised the children that way, they made their own choices after they became of age, that was theirs to do, that of course has to be. Haruko myself and the Creator, I feel we're always pretty close together all through the years. War years, through those, even those, when I'd ask, I would feel a presence kind of a comforting presence. Anytime, anywhere, and it's a good feeling, helps a lot, especially raising a family or doing anything. Haruko and myself and the Creator I feel, were always pretty close together, Haruko I think, felt that way too, Haruko always went to church with me and was baptized at our church.

Now that I've spoken a lot about things we've done together, after the marriage, our marriage I must go back again, seems I'm always doing this. It's going back or kind of, has to be done, because I'm dipping into the past, Haruko's not here, I can feel her presence though. I think she is kind of watching over this writing in her way, playing a big part in these memories flowing through. During my bout with Nephritis and about 6 months stay in the hospital, my tonsils were removed and other treatments performed too. I felt Haruko and the Creator were there with me then too, helping patch things up, when things got serious at times.

The Sands- The Ocean

One day the
Drifting, shifting, loose
Solid, sinking, swallowing
Time moving sands
Of the shores, of the ocean
And it's friend the ocean
Invited me- to
Go and explore
The shores of the far, far away with
The vessels, it's friend, the ocean, and all
It carries nights and days
To the shores of the
Far, far away
And see the world
That it sees, and the
Seas and the oceans, the people,
And the shores of the different lands
Thru the days, and days, today's
And years and days.
And I accepted- traveling
Thru today's and days
Thru years and days.
Enjoying, returning
Thanking the drifting, shifting
Solid, sinking, swallowing
Tide moving sands
Of the ocean
And the ocean
As they tirelessly move
Day by day
Speaking to all
In- its
Mild Thunderous
Addictive way.
To the adventurous, spirit
Of others.
Thru adventures...
Of
The far- far
Faraway.

I felt that way, it helped too, being young only 20 years old and had enlisted at 17 years of age for 3 years of adventure, in military life which I enjoyed, made friends, one person I met we went on the same troop ship was in the same unit in 1948 in Yokohama Japan. We met again in the little church we attend in Salinas California on Lincoln Avenue. The Presbyterian church and see each other now in 2016 each Sunday, life's strange at times isn't it, sometime we reminisce over old times. He also met and married a lady from Yokohama Japan. Adventure calls, when adventure call's most respond and being 20 years of age as I said before in this writing I re-enlisted in the Army for more adventure and also more of the military life as I kind of liked it. Also I kept in touch with Haruko by mail and another way by using the remarkable invention of ham radio through the service club or places where it was available. That's been several years ago, over 60 years now. Much has changed. Ham radios used at those times, didn't cost anything to use also worked pretty good, when the weather was not too bad. Lots of GI's made calls that way stateside, overseas too. But, back then, having reenlisted, taken my furlough home to Michigan and visited my family, I came back to my new assignment at Camp Stoneman in California. It also at that time was a reassignment center. I was assigned to Japan from there in 1948 and the now time was almost June 1950 and I was there again, and… for reassignment again.

Being close to Japan only about 10,000 miles away, I thought why not try to get back over there? I had liked the unit I was with there in Japan. So I got busy looking for something or someway I might get back to the Far East area when there before, I had purchased a bicycle. A lot of people at the time rode bicycles, I just joined the crowd when off duty. I rode all over Yokohama and even out to Camp Zama which was about a 2 hour ride each way, when my unit moved there before I came back to the States, that was fun. Haruko at that time lived in Yokohama, had to see her so I used my bicycle. My mind got to thinking about those times, the good times and Haruko, was disheartened though, after asking some of the GI's That were stationed at Camp Stoneman how long have you guys been here? They said oh, about 2 or 3 years that didn't sound too good to me, I didn't want to stay there. I wanted to get back overseas as soon as possible. There had to be away, so I got busy checking, looking around, and found a unit. The 54th Transportation Heavy Trucking unit, they were training, packing, processing, getting ready soon to leave for the far east and, they thought maybe, Japan. I talked with the first sergeant, he was a nice person too. I told him that I had just reenlisted, just came back from that area and would like to go back, and if his unit could use another body.

Also that I had just came back from my reenlistment furlough, and had not really been assigned to a permanent unit yet. He was interested and wanted to know my MOS. that's the kind of military work a serviceman does. I told him I was a wheeled vehicle mechanic and had done that type of work, on my first enlistment which was the 3 years I had just completed. Also mentioned my high school auto mechanic repair years, I was only 20 years old then. Gee, now am 86 years of age, that seems like a million years ago but brings back, good memories. Lots of water has flowed fast, slow, under the bridge since then. Anyway the first sergeant was interested and wanted to know where I was assigned at Camp Stoneman.

I told him, he replied something like, oh I know that unit, I think he even said he knew the first sergeant there. He told me thanks for coming by, he needed mechanics and that I would probably hear from him soon. I did, in about a week and I was in his unit helping get things ready, and a month or so later was on a troopship, with other ships and vehicles, trailers, and other equipment traveling to the Far East. Just happy and carefree as a young twenty year old guy could be, floating slow across the wide, wide Pacific ocean, to see someone I wanted to see, and to a place where I wanted to be. Love, has lovely silent ways, with lengthy lovely days.

I remember the ship passing under a bridge I think it was the Golden Gate Bridge, might have been the Oakland Bay Bridge. Anyway, I can remember we also passed Alcatraz prison and a GI standing near me watching the California shoreline pass by waved. I asked him who he was waving at, and he said that he was waving at his brother who was in Alcatraz. I told him I'm sorry to hear that,

do you guys keep in touch I asked.

Yes, we do by mail he said I told him that's good, always keep in touch with your brother.

The ship moved on slowly after passing under the bridge and soon, very soon was on wide open ocean past all the shoreline. Then just water, water, deep ocean water for about 2 weeks until we were to get to, Japan that's all we seen. Only we didn't go to Japan, a few days before we got to Japan the ship's Captain announced over the ship's speaker "Attention" everyone. We are now going to Pusan, Korea. That was June of 1950 and things, like the Korean war, were just getting underway in Korea we were soon on our way to Korea.

Alcatraz Island

The Spirit

As the wind, the Spirit came
Not heard, not seen
But understood
In a way that enlightened
The day
And revealed love
Silently, beautifully
Felt, seen, for each-
Quite differently.
Yes, the Spirit came as the wind
As a breath, healing, caring
Giving life, thru love.

I was closer to Haruko though, than I had been for quite a few months. We had always kept in touch by mail. On the ship I came down with something called the shingles. It's some kind of skin disorder. I know it came around my waist area, it's quite painful that was years ago and in August I'll be 87 years of age, I still have the scars. I was treated at the dispensary on the ship and the doctor asked if I'd ever had the chickenpox. I told him I think I had the chicken pox when I was in the 10th grade in high school. Being 20 years old when I got to Korea, it was June of 1950. I graduated from high school in 1947 and 10th grade was in 1945. I would have been fourteen or fifteen years of age when I had the chickenpox. The doctor wrote all this down and gave me something at the time. When we arrived in Korea, the medics put me on a litter with a bunch of other troops where we were all loaded on a smaller boat.

The little boat left its Pusan Harbor and away we went. I thought this is interesting. I asked another GI on a litter close by, where are we going?

He said we're going to a big hospital in Japan.

Miraculous

Miracles we see them
Not in abundance
But they happen every day
They come at times
They come in waves
Sometimes…
Not understood by those
That ask and need
Thru prayer and plead
But in ways that the Creator
Who understands our needs
And answers in ways
Understood in time
With time, our time
As given thru need-
Our need…
With miraculous love.
Miracles….
They happen everyday.

After a few hours we landed in Sapporo Japan and were put on a train and sent to the 8th Station Hospital in Kobe Japan, I couldn't really believe it I was back in Japan. As the train was moving along the coastline of Japan, it was getting dusk, lights were coming on, and I could see lights coming on with Japanese writing from on the train. I didn't expect to come to Japan this way, but I was in Japan and I wanted to come back to Japan again. Thoughts came later, maybe belief in the Creator had something to do with this because little things when needed always seem to fall in place and have continued to do that for years. This has happened for our nearly 60 years of our marriage, and still does thank you Creator. When I got to Kobe hospital, I called Haruko to inform her I was back in Japan. She was surprised and came the next day. Many servicemen were being injured in Korea and getting sent to Kobe hospital. I overheard the hospital medical personnel saying they were short of medical help so I volunteered and told them I would be glad to help out. My case of shingles was healing quite well. They were happy, since I was there as a patient, I could help in many ways.

My job with the hospital lasted about 2 months being a Corporal, I was given a ward with about 90 patients. Of course the medical personnel done most of the medical things I learned how to do some of the small things. Like following the doctor, taking temperatures, writing them down, things like that. changing bandages, matter fact I became a fairly good medic before leaving my brief stay with the hospital there. During the two months that passed, after Haruko got there, I can't remember if I asked her if she wanted to get married. It's too late now because we were married for 58 and a half years. Soon after she got to Kobe though, I got busy fixing the marriage papers because I remembered from having been in Japan before, and seeing friends go through the paperwork of getting married, it's a long process. Much paperwork is required and it takes a long time to complete, if the serviceman is not really serious about the marriage, he might get discouraged. Most of the paperwork I finished during my stay at Kobe hospital, at least, I finished most of the paperwork to get things under way, and that was good. Because Haruko was right there and any medical things needed like x-ray or blood work was easy to do. Doctor checks, to be made all at that time was easy to do also, because I was working at the hospital there.

When my time came to leave the hospital, my unit in Korea found and called for me the hospital folks said, hey you're a mechanic, thanks for the help though."

They were good to me and fixed me up with quite a few days of leave. Haruko and I got on the train in Kobe and rode to Yokohama to our little house there for the leave days I was given then I went back to Korea to my unit there. I was greeted by the motorpool folks with "Vicent, where you been, man? Your toolbox has been waiting for you, also was informed the vehicles roll 24 hours a day, they did too, Korea was at war, our unit was very busy.

I told them I was in the hospital in Kobe Japan and even worked as a medic for a while. they laughed about that. They knew me as a mechanic in our heavy trucking company and I guess they couldn't picture me in a white uniform as a medic. I didn't have any pictures, but I was a medic for about 2 months, that was the last time though, it was nice and I enjoyed it.

When back in Korea during the first few months I finished my marriage papers, it took quite some time because we moved around to several places there. But when I got it all done and the paperwork was ready and I had enough months in Korea to get my R and R, that is rest and recuperation leave because it was wartime in Korea then. I got there when the war was starting in June of 1950. My rest and recuperation leave, was almost 2 weeks leave time, I went back to Japan. Haruko and I were married on the leave in the American Consulate office in Yokohama Japan, November 31st 1951. A friend of mine, I think he was a truck driver in our unit his name was Walter Moorman. We got to Yokohama together on our R& R from Korea, and I remember asking him do you want to be my best man at my wedding?"

Sure, he said I'll do that, what do I have to do?"

I don't know, I told him I've never been married before but we'll find out when the time comes."

Life's Road

Along life's road
There's rocks- there's trails
There's trees- there's green
There's fences- there's clouds
There's blue of sky
There's the silent place
Where memories
Are built too…
Along life's Road
As you, pass thru.

Our Sons
Albert and William Vicent

So I called him to come to Haruko's mothers place for the reception we had. We had a good time and there was lots of food and everything. We took some pictures and he ate a lot of raw fish that type of fish was one of the special dishes served also drank a lot of sake. I told him about it later and he didn't believe me. He ate the fish though, and we had a good laugh. I think it was tuna fish and wasabi. That's been years ago, he left Korea before I did and I haven't seen him since. The military is like that each person seems to go their own separate ways. You do sometimes, but very seldom meet others you've known. The pictures we took of the wedding reception was at Haruko's mothers house. I remember it was all Japanese. The style the wedding was Japanese as you can tell from the picture, Haruko and I are dressed in special kimonos that we rented. It took about an hour or so to get all properly fitted into them. Then my friend came and we had informed him of the time. He and a friend he met are also in the picture. Haruko's familiy is in the picture too. The photographer that took the picture at the time, did not use electronic flash, I think he used carbide or something like that. I know the camera and all except the lens was covered I think he stuck his head under the cover too. He pulled something, there was a real bright flash, and the picture was taken. The picture came out good, and that's what matters, lots of material, was not available or even produced at that time in 1951, so people used what was available to do what had to be done.

After the marriage I returned to Korea to finish my tour of duty there and came back through Japan and was assigned the YMC, Yokohama Motor Command for 2 or 3 months to get things ready to bring my wife Haruko back to America. Yokohama Motor Command was about a 30 minute bicycle ride from our little house in Yokohama. I would ride my bicycle to work almost every morning sometime I would ride the streetcar, but most of the time I would ride my bicycle it was springtime. The cherry blossoms were blooming and it was a beautiful time of the year in Japan.

The Best

Do the very best
You can do, all
The time
Is always right
To do
The best you can do.
So always
Do the very best
You can do- all the time.

When Haruko and I went to America, her brother used my bicycle as a bicycle taxi cab in Yokohama, there was not many automobiles like there are now but there were quite a few bicycle taxi cabs. A small, light little sidecar was fastened to the bicycle it only had one wheel the rider could move along quite easily with one person in the little side car. Haruko's brother used the bicycle that way frequently. It was versatile because the bicycle could be disconnected from the taxi cab portion quite easily. The GI's used bicycle taxicabs quite a lot. sometime more than one person would jump in and would have to help the driver push up rather steep inclines. Then they would then jump back in and a way they would go, everyone seemed happy.

Those two or three months I stayed in Yokohama getting papers and everything ready to bring Haruko back to America were really nice too, especially after the Korean War months. We stayed in our little house in Yokohama and Haruko fixed my lunch. I would a ride to work every morning, back home again on my bicycle every evening, it was nice kind of like a sort of honeymoon. Sometimes we went around to many of the old places I knew when stationed in Yokohama before with the 76th AAA, but the unit had moved to Zama Japan before I returned to America in 1949. Now new Japanese buildings were in its place, Japan was rebuilding rapidly, to become highly industrialized.

The Night

The Stars they light like banners the night
The moon there too, it lights as one- the night
Together the stars, the moon... light night
With mysterious light
That light's with love most earth at night
With Heavenly
Starlight and moonlight.

Hours

The hours they move quiet- going by
Like clouds move in the sky
I think maybe- the sun, it watches
Tho... when it brings night

As it sets low, in the sky.
So all, will know
The hours- have passed
Quiet, by.

The Years

You liked what I liked
I liked what you liked
Mostly you did what I did
Mostly I did what you did
We talked things through, most times
Before the sun was thru
Or before the sun went down
The best way to end the day
You understood what I understood
I went where you went
You went where I went
We understood in our way
The years passed by, a happy way.
We're happy now, in our own way
I guess we done

We did what we done
We're not done yet
And we've done it together, with love
And we done it thru
The years.

Yesterday

Yesterday... came with the sun and-
Stayed with the sun all day
And when
The sun went away the day-
Went away too.
But...
I still remember, yesterday some
And the sun-
When yesterday...went thru.

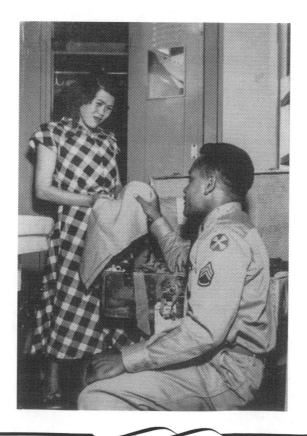

But passing the old areas brought back memories and memories are nice. The time passed quickly and I got everything in order to bring Haruko to America. One morning we went to Yokohama port and loaded on the troop ship. I believe that it was called the MM Patrick. Haruko waved at her parents and family that came to see her off and together she and I set off to start a new life in a brand new country for Haruko. The United States of America and a new family life for both of us. Haruko, I think enjoyed the trip she got a little seasick the first few days but was all right the rest of the trip. It took almost 2 weeks to make the crossing I think we landed in Seattle Washington, traveled by bus to my new assignment in Fort Ord California. Where I stayed for about two or three years working as an instructor teaching wheeled vehicle maintenance.

Our Way

Tho she is gone forever
Forever gone away
In yonder cemetery
Put there soon, 2 years ago
To stay
We have our conversations
Some may not think
Tis so
But we understand
At least I do
In our own special way
She speaks as if before
Almost as much of old
To me it's so- and of
The old.
Means much in silence
And fill the space
Special...she filled for
Nearly sixty years, before
She left- to forever stay
Tho she is gone forever
We now have conversations
At least for now... Sometime
Our way.
Our Silent Way.

Doves

Two Doves just landed
Here together they flew
As they came by
And together they stay
They must know
Each other.
At least it seems so
Today
Two doves
The two doves
That flew here
So quiet…
As they came today
It seems…
Dove's speak, dove's way, silently.

Haruko and I got Govt. living quarters in a place called Ord. village on Ft. Ord. The buildings were old converted army barracks but they were OK and we liked them. That is where Haruko got her first experience of American home life in a real American type house even though it was a converted army barracks. it had or was arranged in American house style. The Army gave us some housing items to use like chairs, table, beds, and one or two dressers. This was great because we only had Haruko's suitcase with her items and my duffel bag with my things. So the items the Army let us use really came in good. Of course we got more household items of our own later, but those military loan items really helped to get us started. We were definitely new to living American family style I lived with my family as a child before and Haruko and I had a little house in Japan, but that was Japanese style she done her cooking on a Hibachi, she was very good cook and rapidly learned many American dishes.

Those combined with her knowledge of Japanese cooking, she very soon had knowledge of both worlds mastered her way. Haruko was a wonderful cook she could never get me to like soy sauce, of course she loved it. She prepared most of her dishes with it but my food she prepared without it. The children all loved soy sauce only I didn't. Haruko over our 58 and a half years of marriage prepared my food without soy sauce. That seemed no trouble for her she just done things that way. Most of the brides from Japan, Haruko's friends have a little cookbook of many American recipes and how to prepare them. It was written in English and Japanese. I think it was a given to them in Japan because of most of our friends seem to have the same little book. I think after all these years it's still here in the house somewhere. Haruko found the little book to be quite helpful and I've seen her use it a lot. When we moved into the housing area at Fort Ord California- Ord village, a warrant officer and his wife can't remember their names, but they were nice people. His wife became very good friends with Haruko and showed her many things about American housekeeping and the American way of life. They lived right next door to us. They also showed her how to use the gas type cooking range.

When Haruko went to use it herself though, she paused too long after she turned the gas on. I guess she didn't have a match close by when she turned the gas on so when she struck the match the gas had built up and when the gas ignited it shook the kitchen area she said. But in spite of that, when I got home from work that evening she had everything prepared she didn't let the mishap bother her. Haruko became very familiar with the American way of life very quickly and enjoyed our time that Fort Ord. Haruko had worked at fish markets in Japan and she said she wanted to work at the Monterey sardine place processing sardines which was operating at that time at Fisherman's Wharf in Monterey California. She worked a couple months there. That was enough time for her to spend there. I think she got tired of it too, we sure had a lot of those little silverfish during those about two months. I think the fish kind of disappeared from the area now Fisherman's wharf is more of a visitor's area.

We were to have had a child at Fort Ord but Haruko had a miscarriage we had children later though. In the Autumn of 1952 our first year at Fort Ord I think it was during our first year. Haruko and I went to Michigan to visit my family I think we went by bus (the Greyhound) and that was a long, long ride. Haruko got to see much of America from California to Michigan and back to California. She met my family, we all had a good time together, my mother was really fond of Haruko and came the following summer to visit us at Fort Ord. She came by train and stayed about two weeks, we all had a good time that was the first time my mother had ever traveled that far from Michigan and also for her to see the ocean. After about 2 years, maybe a little more or less, I received orders to go to Alaska, Haruko remained at Ord village.

I drove an old car I had purchased to Seattle Washington and put it on the ship sent it to Alaska then. away I went to Alaska Was assigned to a medical unit there as their motor sergeant. The unit was on Ladd Air Force Base in Fairbanks Alaska. I found a little house off base there, right away and sent for Haruko. She came very soon, as soon as she got everything ready and cleared at Fort Ord. We were only away from each other maybe 2 or 3 months. Our oldest son was born in Alaska on August 3rd 1954. He is now 62 years of age, years move along. Alaska is a beautiful place, very cold in the winter and quite warm in the summer.

Haruko got her American citizenship in Fairbanks Alaska. She and I studied for her test together for quite some time. Then went to the place in Fairbanks Alaska to take the test and she passed, becoming an American citizen. She was quite happy because she and I had studied together for a long time preparing for the test. At the time I think we were two knowledgeable people of citizenship material. We adopted a child from Japan, she came to us in Alaska shortly before my tour finished there. We had known her mother in Japan, the child's mother passed away before we adopted the child. Her name was Kuniko and we gave her the middle name of Marie, Kuniko Marie Vicent. She got her citizenship about the same time as Haruko, also the middle name was added, she was then 8 years old.

Where my tour was finished in Alaska, I received orders for Fort Lewis Washington where my second son William Henry Vicent was born at Madigan General Hospital in Tacoma Washington, on November 30th 1956. We also purchased a home there at the time for $4,000 and kept it for several years. It was located at 1245 South Hosmer Street, I think it's still there. It was an old home then, much older now of course, was still pretty solid when we purchased it though. We lived there for quite a while sometime it would snow a little in the winter months of the year but wouldn't last long. The snow would melt in a week or even less, the children were old enough to make a snowman when enough snow fell. One time. I think Haruko and I helped them a little. Haruko enjoyed that, I think she said that was the first snow man she had ever helped make, because in Japan there was no snow in the part where she lived.

In Alaska we didn't make snowmen, when we left our son was only about 3 or 4 months old and our daughter came in the summer when we were leaving just a few weeks before we left Alaska for Fort Lewis Washington. Our daughter had fun helping make a snowman in Washington. Kuniko had not experienced snow because she came from the Tokyo Yokohama area of Japan. It gets cold there but rarely snows much, our family had fun making the Tacoma snowman. Haruko enjoyed that experience, I think she sent her family in Japan one of the pictures of her standing by our house, by the snowman. The old house we bought in Tacoma Washington also had a separate garage not attached to the house. I painted the trim, steps, porch, and other areas I could paint on the house. Haruko helped also, she enjoyed doing things like that. We painted the garage and trimmed it in green, green was Haruko's favorite color. The old house also had a pear tree in the backyard that looked old but always produced lots of really sweet large delicious pears.

Haruko canned some of the pears I can't remember how she learned the American way of canning, but she learned and did a good job of it too. Most any place we traveled, any base we traveled to service men would be married to someone from another country. Of course there always were many more American brides. But Haruko had many Japanese friends married to servicemen. She quickly learned, that being a service man's wife and traveling as a serviceman's family there are many places, people are from. Just about all over the world as long as they meet the strict military standards to become military. They all then live together, as one big family. Haruko was always a friendly remarkable person, she seemed to get along with almost everyone. Of course if she would happen to meet someone in the PX, post exchange commissary, or some other place from her country that spoke her language, naturally they would quite soon find each other's address phone number and all. Friendships many friendships were made that way, that lasted for years. Some of the friends from in the military I still keep in contact with those families not many, because I retired from the service in 1972, the time now is 2016, that was quite a few years ago.

When we married in the early 1950's we married in 1951, quite a lot of men were marrying and bringing their wives with them. We would encounter people from all over the world. Haruko had many Japanese friends she could converse with and when the children came along she was plenty busy being a housewife, a military housewife which is a little different but not too much from being a civilian housewife. Only in the military, the family has to be ready to move every few years. Haruko had no trouble that way, in fact we enjoyed the military, our meeting while in the military, our marriage, raising our family, from childhood all the way, to their early adult years. Haruko and I and the children have always kept and speak often of those times, even though it's been years ago, we reminisce think sometime, of the old military days.

Of course Haruko isn't with us anymore except in memory, pictures, etc. I can still remember, always will, the good old days I would save up a lot of furlough days and when the children got out of school Christmas vacation or something, take a vacation. Especially when we were on the west coast and wanted to visit my mother and family on the east coast. Like when I was stationed at Fort Lewis Washington and took a furlough to visit my mother in Michigan, the children were small, but we were young and adventurous too.

Haruko and I talked about the trip, we had a pretty good old car it was a 1953 Ford we bought when I coming back from my Alaska tour of duty. It wasn't new, but met my mechanical automotive knowledge as being or would be okay for the trip. One thing I remembered of doing I believe it was that time. I had seen somewhere an advertisement of a car the back of the driver's bench type seat could be laid down for sleeping in the car while traveling. In those time's people would pull over and rest or even sleep a few hours at the roadside stops of course times have changed and now it wouldn't be safe. Maybe it wasn't then, but we never had any trouble. The family and I before she passed would sometime talk about the old times of traveling across the United States, and laugh about those odd things the Vicent family done during their cross-country travels.

Back to Preparing the auto my old 53 Ford at that time. It was a good car and seemed to kind of understand, all the odd, different things I done to and with it. It was a very patient and good car with me, never did give any big trouble. We kept it for about 12 years and took it to Okinawa Japan. Stayed there five years and had it checked over and brought it back drove it all the way across country again to Michigan and back to Aberdeen Proving Ground in Maryland. There and sold it to another GI who took it to Wisconsin, it was a good old car. I'm telling what was finally done with the car, we still had it, in this part of the story. At that time though, we were getting ready to take my furlough to Michigan with it, I had read about a car that was made with a bench type driver's seat that could be lowered to make a bed for sleeping and being a little mechanical minded I fixed the back of my old Ford so it would do that too. Haruko came and watched me for a while and remarked what are you doing to the car?

I told her," I'm making it so we can sleep in it."

It's too small she said, where will the children sleep?

I told her I will make a hammock on top and rest one end on top of the dash, and the other end on top of the backseat."

Haruko thought it was kind of a goofy idea but it worked, and the kids thought it was fun. The kids slept on hammocks on top and Haruko and I slept on the lowered back seat on the bottom. Maybe one night, next night we would catch a motel. At the time of travel, many of the highways were still gravel traveling across country they were still good highways though. Also on the old Ford its V8 engine was designed so that a can of beans or soup could be placed beside an engine mount close to the hot engine manifold's and after about forty or fifty miles of driving we could stop and remove a can or cans then, with some sandwiches have a pretty good driving type meal. We used to heat c-rations on the old GI trucks that way during the Korean War.

Haruko, the kids, and I would sometime think back at those times and say, "Wow. We made it and had fun too."

That's what life's all about now ain't it now, oh one other thing we used to do sometime when we traveled. There used to be sold mostly in camping equipment places, a little folding type stove with a little can of flammable mixture that burned real hot. Campers used it for frying eggs and bacon or cooking little things on. It was called called canned heat, we used to use that sometimes at road stops, to cook little things, it worked good too. Haruko used it much like her little Hibachi she had used in Japan not too many years before our famed old cross country trips. I guess I put the family through those kind of traveling times because I guess it did save a little on motel bills, but way back in my mind even then I always liked camping and doing that type of thing. I liked roughing it, camping, still do. No damage was done, just memories. We always carried a nice ice box with lots of food in it. When we stopped at motels, we would always get a motel with kitchen facilities, where Haruko always made her rice, we would always have rice in the icebox, rice cooked and ready in the icebox.

We've done quite a lot of tent camping after I retired from the Army and took the children and grandchildren as well. We stayed at KOA Campgrounds, they were always a lot of fun and they are in a lot of places across America. One time we rented a cabin in the Lake Tahoe area of California it was nice cabin in a nice area. I believe in the month of June, spring time of the year. When we got there was putting our things in the cabin, and unloading the car. Some people were walking by it was getting slightly dark toward evening time. they said are "You going to stay in that cabin tonight?"

I replied, yes. we plan on staying here."

They just looked with a kind of amazed look on their face and kept walking. Haruko asked what did those people want. I told her they just asked if we were going to stay here and I told them yes, we rented the place. She said why did they ask that, do you think everything is ok?"

I told, yes, I'm sure everything will be ok.

Haruko, her mother, and I, stayed in the cabin for maybe 3 or 4 days.

Invite

If a ghost came over
And sat by you
Today
What would you
To the ghost
Say
Would you hold
The ghost hand
And say to the ghost
Let's go get
A pizza
And some
Popcorn too
The ghost might
Like you
To say that too
And if you did
The ghost might
Go with you
And say
Thank you, then
Invite you
To a visit
With the ghost
At the
Ghost house
A real, real
Ghost house
Try it do it

Too
If a ghost
Comes and
Sits with you
Anytime
Any day.
I dare you to,
This do.

That cabin gave a strange experience at night, the first night we were there the cabin had an upstairs area, I think one or two rooms were upstairs. It was a nice cabin. But on the stairway it seemed someone or something was there, trying to say something, like someone had done something. I could not see anyone. I just got that impression and feeling, it was strange. It bothered my mother-in-law too. She was sleeping in a room downstairs beside our room, she rushed over to our room, about the time these things or thoughts started happening, and stayed in our room very frightened and wide eyed. I attempted to use the telephone when all this was happening but it was inoperable. I made sure the windows and doors were secure, we had a nice vacation. It was just a strange cabin. In the rooms upstairs they always seemed cold, and unfriendly maybe it was haunted I don't know, maybe it was just our imagination. Maybe that's why those folks walking by when we were unloading the car said what they did, we'll never know.

We laughed about it later but Haruko and her mother said to never rent that cabin again it was fun though, we had a good time. My camping or my love of camping took the family through an old camper vehicle, my little Volkswagen pop-up camper which I really loved. Kept it for over 20 years until one night Haruko and I were in the house watching the television, there was a loud crash in the front of our house. I told Haruko' my goodness someone must have had an automobile accident."

We looked outside through the window and someone had ran into the rear of my Volkswagen Camper. Parked next to the curb in front of our house. Then backed his vehicle up and tried to get away. But his vehicle had been damaged quite extensively, it was pouring liquid from the vehicle's radiator all over the street. We immediately called the police and tracked the vehicle right to the house where it was parked, someone there was given a ticket. But everyone moved from the house about a week later. The uninsured motorist part of my auto insurance gave me something for the VW Camper. Haruko and I talked about the old Volkswagen quite a lot after it had been so severely damaged sitting right in front of our home that night. She wondered how people could do something like that and just practically disappear. I could only tell her the world is full of all types of people. That person did receive a ticket but that was the last I have heard of the matter. We were perhaps fortunate this state has uninsured motorist Insurance to help cover such matters. I really hated losing that old Volkswagen camper. Haruko I, and our children, and grandchildren camped with it several times. It was a type of vehicle that was short, because the engine was in the rear. Had lots of room inside, it could sleep four adult people. Also had a hammock that fit over the driver's seat where a child, could sleep. It was really good for camping hauling lots of things. I used it too for driving to work every day. It was a classic vehicle not many of that type of vehicle are still around. We had it for over 20 years, its existence in our lives finally drifted mostly, but not entirely out of our lives like things in life do. Of course I'll always remember it, like the shadow from a standing tree, just look, and it's always there.

Enough about Haruko myself and the family camping experiences for now, but before we leave our bit about camping I must write about our camping thing. Our oldest son Charlie when his children were small, bought a house trailer that he pulled with his quite large SUV vehicle. We used to go quite a few places together with an old motor home I purchased, my younger son and his family would go along. Between the two vehicles there was adequate room for everyone. Sometime brought along Haruko's Japanese friend we met the family while in the military in Okinawa. She lived in I think, in Pittsburg California, and would come to visit Haruko in Salinas quite often. The ladies would get together camping, we certainly had some good times. The ladies, our families, grandchildren, everybody altogether camping.

Sitting around the campfire, cooking hot dogs, steak, corn, almost anything desired. Oh yes chicken too, seems like things cooked over a campfire with everyone talking, laughing and having a good time with family, friends, the food just tastes super. Also Charles two boys both attained Eagle Scout. Charles is my oldest son. He is also a scoutmaster and teaches others of the scoutmaster profession. Our younger son gave us two granddaughters. They are not too interested in camping, but did accompany us camping when they were younger. Our younger son Henry would a rent a small house trailer and take it sometimes where we camped.

After I retired from the military I quite soon got into camping included the family through the tent stage into a Volkswagen, pop up camper. an old motor home when the VW van was demolished by the late-night hit and run driver. I have another camper big enough for me and I still go camping about every one and a half, or two or three months at a place called Laguna Seca about 10 to 12 miles away. Laguna Seca is a large racetrack where many races are held and people from all over come to race their vehicles from bicycles, motorcycles, to all type of automobiles. The place has about a hundred or more camping spots. I go when there are no races scheduled. It's quiet a place then with electric hookups at all. I have a special spot I take my writing equipment and just write, write, write having a wonderful time. Like right now I'm writing this book about my memories of, Haurko and I. Which will probably be the title of this book, which just may be mostly completed there. Depends on how the imagery comes and goes, right now it's filtering through the memory banks quite well.

When I was stationed at Fort Lewis in Tacoma, Washington, Russia had sent up a little space module and I think it was called Sputnik and soon the space program was a pretty big thing. Where I was in the military, they started looking for people with a certain score in their records in certain areas to train them in electronics and, I had a favorable score. So I put in to be trained in that field and was accepted. Very soon off I went to Fort Monmoth, New Jersey to be trained in electronics. This is the field I stayed in for the rest of my military time. That was about 15 years total in electronics. Then, I had served about 10 years making 25 years military time when I retired. Electronics was good, and interesting. For the training I had to leave Haruko and the family in the $4,000 house we bought in Tacoma Washington and off I went to Fort Monmoth, New Jersey to school. I met some of my old friends there we had known at Fort Ord California with Japanese wives Had not seen them for years, haven't seen them since, but they were there. That's been over 60 years ago now. I think I gave Haruko their phone number and they corresponded by phone over the years. We kept in touch for a while but gradually lost contact with each other.

When I finished the course at New Jersey, I was sent to Redstone Arsenal in Huntsville Alabama for training in the missile field. The course was quite lengthy, so when we got a Christmas break from school which was for about two weeks more or less. I found out before the break that housing was available for those who wanted to bring their families, because the school was quite lengthy. I wanted to bring my family so I put in, and got housing. When Christmas break from school came, another student with a car was driving to Tacoma Washington and wanted three or four others to ride along help on the gas price. I got it on the group came back to Washington, picked up the family and loaded them up in my old 53 ford and headed for Huntsville, Alabama. I already had living quarters so that was no problem. When I finished the school, I was kept at the school as permanent party. We stayed at Redstone Arsenal Huntsville Alabama for nearly six years. It was a nice assignment and I liked it. Another missile school system started while I was at Redstone, I heard it might be going to the Far East. I put in for the school, being already there, having housing, everything was okay. I was accepted for the school and it was another very lengthy school. When the school finished, there was a unit going to Okinawa. It was not Japan, but it was close.

I put in for the unit and got accepted. I can't remember, it's been so many years, nearly 60 or more ago. Whether I left the family at Redstone Salashan housing kind of an on post, off post, housing unit Lots of military personnel stayed there. Or whether I had the family go back to our place in Tacoma. I think I left the family at Redstone Arsenal housing because we were informed housing in Okinawa could be obtained off base quite quickly. When we got there, I found a house very quick and I had sent the car when I left for Okinawa. It was there soon after I arrived the family arrived soon also. Picked up the family and took them to our little house in Okinawa. The house was located in a place called Kadena near Kadena gate # 1 house #245 Sunabe in Okinawa.

The little house was very near the ocean, of course everywhere is near the ocean in Okinawa. The island of Okinawa is about 60 miles long and 15 miles wide. That's the dimensions I was told, but Okinawa was okay and a nice place we liked it. We stayed there 9 years altogether. 5 years 1 time and 4 years another. I kept extending my tour because it was so near Japan. Haruko and our family could visit Japan most anytime. Her family visited us in Okinawa quite often, we really enjoyed Okinawa. It was a small island, but we usually put ten thousand or more miles on our car every year because we were always going on a picnic or somewhere because the beach was everywhere. When we were there, the military had nice clubs, good food, good entertainment and we enjoyed it, we really enjoyed Okinawa. The residents of Okinawa could speak and understand Japanese, Haruko's language pretty good, most spoke English fairly well, also had their own language. But because they spoke Japanese language, and because she could travel with no trouble there, with most of the stores carrying Japanese products, Haruko was right at home. There was school for the children in Okinawa also, the military had good schools with military colored school buses to pick up and return the children through all grades, elementary through high school. All children went through most of their Elementary and through high school years now that I think of it. Our oldest son Albert Charles did graduate in Okinawa at Kubasaki High School in 1972 before we came back to America, I then retired from the Army at Fort Ord California.

The American Legion and the VFW had excellent clubs for the military when we were there we often went. The food was excellent, and day time till early evening we could take the children. All weekend when I didn't have duty and was free to be with the family, we often went on a picnic to the beach or somewhere. Or maybe just rambling around on Okinawa, when our day's travel was finished, we would usually stop by the American Legion, VFW Club and had a meal or went to the movies. There were also very nice Okinawan and military clubs on Okinawa we frequented the Topper NCO club it was a very nice club. Of course that was many years ago having left there to retire 1972 and this is 2016. Quite a few years have passed since those times, imagine much as changed. I know we have, the memories are still there and they are good memories. We also saw quite a few celebrities that came to visit the troops. They would come to the clubs and entertain we and our friends would go see them.

I can remember seeing Tommy Dorsey, Louis Jordan, Bob Hope, and others. So many I can't remember their names now. Haruko the family and I had good times on Okinawa traveling through the many adventures together, along life's road. Because Okinawa is so close to Japan, Haruko's mother, her brothers and their families used to come visit by ship. It was always a good vacation for them and was a nice opportunity for Haruko to spend quality time with her family. We would take them to the clubs there and show them around the island. We always had a good time together. They and Haruko seemed to always look forward to those family visits, we also would visit Japan almost every year while on Okinawa. That was one of the reasons I stayed there so long, also because I liked the duty and the area. Haruko was close to her family, the family was happy if work is ok, and the family is happy, most everything else is ok.

Travel along life's road can be pretty smooth and make time seem to just glide kind of silent by. It did and nine years went by and the children grew up to almost through the teenage years. In fact, our daughter did, we didn't bring her back when the family came back the second time to Okinawa. She was working for the telephone company and later got married. Has given us grandchildren, great and great, great grandchildren. Of course we have grandchildren from each of our three children. Back to Okinawa, kind of got off the subject each year we would go to Japan from Okinawa, when I built up my furlough days. It was quite easy to go to the Kadena air base and catch space available to fly most anywhere. At the time a lot of flights were traveling to Japan, to Tachikawa, and Yokota, airbase where we wanted to go. I would put my name on a list at the airbase with how many seats needed and wait till my name came up on the list. When a flight was scheduled to go with my amount of empty open seats, away we would go.

When we got to our place in Japan I would put my name on the list and the date I wanted to catch a flight back to Okinawa go to the military airport in Japan with the family and wait for a plane out. We usually got out pretty good most times, sometime we would get held up in Japan especially if a typhoon was passing through. One time we got held up I think for three days we were lucky though, the guesthouse on the base there had some open rooms available so we stayed there until the flights resumed again. We eventually got back to Okinawa, during our wait we even got some SOS in the cafeteria. That's creamed beef on toast Haruko could make it too. The GI's had another name for it, those are good memories, the children and I sometimes talk about those old times. The space available on flights were usually on C-130 planes, they were quite large and could take a big load or a lot of cargo each way. They also usually had quite a lot of passenger seating that was open that we waiting space A folks gladly filled. The children still now fondly remember those family space A flights from Okinawa to Japan. I'm even writing about them now, gosh. it's only been about fifty years or more ago, and that's only a number.

Space A space available flights were free and if one was not in a big rush was always fun, even my family got to kind of enjoying it. A lot of servicemen when I was on active duty traveled that way. Of course if they were in a big hurry to be someplace they bought a ticket, otherwise many would travel Space A. we didn't always travel by C-130 planes, though a lot of them were flying when we wanted to go, where we wanted to go with open seats so we got on them. Sometime Haruko and I would catch a C-141 airplane. They were a large plane. I can remember we had to climb many steps to the tail section to get our seats. Once in the air the plane traveled rapidly toward its destination from Travis Air Base in California to I believe Yokota Air Base in Japan gave a nice smooth rapid flight. In my memory, I think our return flight from Japan that time was by a C-141 plane.

One time when Haruko the family, and I were stationed in Okinawa, I had been there for a long time and wanted to see my family in America. I had not been back to see my mother and other family members for a while. So I took a furlough put in for Space A flight for only myself. I left Haruko and the family at our government housing there and caught a tanker type airplane that could refuel another airplane in flight, it had a few open seats and I got a seat. The plane stopped by Guam on the way, that's a real small place we landed at a Marine base in California, can't remember the name of it, had a nice flight, all the way. I think I got a hop out of there also, to somewhere in Detroit Michigan or the Ohio area, can't remember now. I was also lucky on my return trip, to Haruko and the family in Okinawa. I got another Space A flight directly to Okinawa it was on a flight called a charter flight. A civilian passenger airplane carrying military people, waitresses, food, everything. I really lucked out that time, first class all the way, the plane stopped off for a short time in Japan and then on to Okinawa Naha Airport.

When I got back to Haruko and the family in Okinawa, they were happy, and all was okay there. Haruko and I traveled many miles on Space A flights. One time we went from Okinawa to Taiwan and stayed a few days, and looked around Taiwan. Our housemaid looked after the children at our government quarters in Okinawa while we were gone. We had a nice time, Taiwan was an interesting place. This book though, being mainly about Haruko and I, must also cover many of those many things as can be remembered from when we met in 1948, I think it was about February of 1948. From then till now is quite a span of time to try and recall some of the small things that captivate take up, make up the really, really interesting, happy, sad, mediocre, just bearable, and bearable, livable days, of days that make up life. I'll try to recall some of those days now as I can think of, and remember them as they come to me. Now and through the remainder of this book. I'm sure they won't all filter through at the same time, because our 58 and a half years of marriage covered quite a few days, that's the 3 years of time from February 1948 when we first met, to our marriage November 30, 1951 in Yokohama Japan. All together that covers nearly 61 years, of days that made up life our lives together happy bearable, and where they could, thorough and with each other, create, also continue to create in the 61 years, of love for each other.

Even now over six years after her passing I still have her clothes as she left them hanging in her clothes closet area where she kept them and in the manner she hung them. I may have written of this before, some say that's not a good to carry grief so long, but to me it's not grief, it to me it's just memories, good memories I want to keep that way. When the time comes, and it's right for me to dispose of things, at that time when feelings are complete. I'll do just that. Memories created of our togetherness Haruko and I will always be there as a soft summer moonlight night, memorable, ever pleasant to recall. We always tried to keep Communication open between the two of us, that we felt was very important. Many times, at the days end we would take an evening walk, discuss things, it's strange how togetherness, a slow walk, eventide, and just ordinary friendly talk does wonders. It's also good exercise.

When the children came along we would include them on our walk sometime or after they went to bed we could sit together, find a little time for togetherness. We always found that to be important even if not much was being said, it just that seemed like it kind of at times puts a certain smooth good feeling and, without a lot of words, also did good at times.

Communication if we let it, kind of teaches us that way, we had our good and bad times, but we always would try and slow down, slow each other down, gradual, with calm good common sense. Things always worked out, we always created a lot of good memories along the way. I didn't realize it then, but it seems to surface now with a rearward glance at the good and the bad. We done it, it has to be viewed it's there, it enabled us to be where we are it's with us.

We chose each other as partners, we lived our lives, even when only things like eating peanuts, popcorn, walking together through a park, or a suburban area of town. I can remember when I first met Haruko in Yokohama Japan in early February of 1948. At the time there were a lot of little places that cook things outside along the sidewalks like frying small fish in huge frying pans maybe two and a half feet in diameter. It seemed just bubbling with oil, hot oil at night. These little places would be lit with soft of light quite visible maybe of carbide, but not real bright like now, it was right after the war. Anyway fresh fish being fried is good anywhere, it gives off a good odor, wakes up the appetite. Also close by sweet potatoes would be roasting on someone's little outdoor cookery or maybe fresh corn depending on the season or availability. Haruko would usually get some fresh fried fish, small fish maybe what we would call a bluegill, sand dab, or that type of fish. She also would get roasted sweet potatoes, and put them in her little shopping bag, basket or fur-roo-shik-ka, a cloth tied by its four corners to hold items. Usually we would continue walking if it was a nice day. just having a good time. The area and the country was new. even the day there, was new to me then. It was always enjoyable to go shopping with Haruko at these little sidewalk markets that way, it was different. When we would get to her place with the fish, sweet potatoes, she usually always would cook rice on a little hibachi. She would then warm the fish and sweet potatoes, what a delicious meal, what a memory, to remember. The Creator creates many things that remains for us through the years, that seems as only yesterday, but was years ago. Because 1948 was when Haruko and I first met that was 68 years ago now, for it is the year of 2016 today. Those memories, and the years did not harm them a bit. They came for a reason, they are beautiful like sunlight, soft rain, moonlight, rainbows, are, and will be forever treasured by me.

Haruko was always a good cook and soon learned my likes and dislikes of Japanese foods before and after our marriage and together we blended our lengthy years of marriage she knew my American food choices and cooked food that way. Which did not cause her much problems because she knew I never liked soy sauce as she all over most of her food, so she fixed my foods with no soy sauce, except some like o-sem-bi was ok. The foods were mostly all the same otherwise, only no soy sauce on mine. Fish vegetables most all vegetables, not Japanese potatoes, other vegetables most all were okay. Just no soy sauce on them for me. fish all okay, octopus no, didn't care for those but Haruko liked them. Fish with lots of bones, small fish like mackerel when I eat them. I have to eat them slow, pick out all the bones and Haruko would help me take out the bones. She and Her friends, if they were dining with us at home, or a restaurant would laugh at my being so careful with the fish bones. But that's my fish eating style, I would remind them I don't like small fish bones to get stuck in my throat.

Haruko and Her friend had no trouble eating fish, especially with the bones, she and they were experts in that field or so it seemed to be. When I got to Japan I ate my first koo-ji-die whale meat, when I got there in 1948, it was still in the markets. Was later removed because the whales were declared being among the endangered species. But I got to eat whale meat, it was delicious I liked it. It's taste to me was something like beef or at least the part I ate to me was. It was in the fish markets in large square pieces at that time. I also remember going with Haruko to her birthplace in Yamanashi-ken Japan, a lot of grapes are raised there. When we went, we traveled on a steam powered train, a steam locomotive pulled the train. It was a beautiful trip through the countryside traveling there from Yokohama. We got there stayed a few days with her relation, they had a very nice house with a straw top on the home. Not many like that anymore except maybe in pictures or perhaps way in the country.

Anyway, when in bed the first night, I asked Haruko what is that noise?

She laughed and said I should have told you, that is the silkworms. Lots of people raise them here for the silkworm larvae which is used to make silk."

That was an interesting trip to Haruko's birthplace. When I was later stationed in Okinawa and would visit Japan we took the children to visit her birthplace and they enjoyed it too. It was always fun buying items of furniture with Haruko, we would always try to include each other in the purchase it seemed now that I think of it. She would ask me before the final purchase, are you sure you like it? Maybe about the color or something, and to just sit down, lay down if the purchase was a bed, or sofa. She rarely said comfortable, that was not a word she used very much. Of course I would usually most always ask the same of her, on purchases like that. That way perhaps it's more fun and the good or bad of the purchase made to later realize together. We always made most big purchases of things like furniture when we were together. Haruko kind of insisted on it or seemed we just made a habit of doing that, I really miss Haruko we made purchase of things and we always done much together. Because we almost always went places together, through the years we always went together, when you would see one of us you usually, seen the other close by. Raising the family also through the years as most purchasing, was done together. That togetherness Haruko and I did it was great seemed like she insisted on it, I really miss Haruko.

Raising the family, when punishment time came of a child's misdeeds of something done wrong, if Haruko spotted the wrongdoing of the child first and the something done wrong was small she took care of it and that was all. If the something done wrong was big, she informed the child, when your father comes back we will talk about this some more. The children knew this, and I always have done the same. That way we always knew pretty much what the children were doing, perhaps not everything, hardly any parent knows everything their children do. What is important is to know most things, the important things to be known to properly raise a child. Haruko insisted on that and we both agreed, we made sure the children knew that Haurko done a very good job of, the children knew that. She got the word to the children very quick if they done or committed and a misdeed, Haruko soon found out about it. I would often ask her how did you know?

She would usually answer I know, I know. and she was most always right.

The children very quickly learned that and passed their growing years and even their teenage years on to adult years with some, but little trouble.

Christmas

Next week on this day
Will be Christmas Day, Christmas Day
On this day it will be
Christmas Day
One week away
Some will be happy- some sad
Little children usually glad.
On…
Merry Christmas
Merry Christmas
Merry Christmas Day and…
Next week on this day
It will be-
Merry Christmas Day.

While the children were growing, it was always great fun preparing for Easter egg preparation, coloring the eggs, egg hunts and all. Christmas too was always fun, Haruko always had great fun purchasing presents each child might like, of course we did it together. But she seemed to get so much fun from Christmas. The presents and all, getting the tree, decorating it with the family, and wrapping the presents, watching the children open their presents. She seemed to get such enjoyment from seeing the children so happy at Christmas with their presents, and communicating with their family and friends, on the holidays were new to her. Japan had similar days but different dates with different meanings, now Christmas is a pretty big day in Japan too. Just remembered one time now maybe twenty years more or less ago, my two sons, one son Charles brought his family. The other son, Haruko and I caught plane and away we went to Japan for about 2 weeks to visit Haruko's family. We had a nice time, a very nice time. The weather was nice also, only quite warm as it was the month of July. While we were there, a part of that trip we went to the city of Kyoto. I believe it was in Kyoto we roamed around quite a lot one night just walking the streets with many people that walk the city streets. Just gazing and talking and having a good family late evening walk. I remember we stopped in one little restaurant, Haruko's brother knew Kyoto quite well at least much better than any of our group and he served as our guide that evening. While walking we seen this one little restaurant and went in my brother-in-law found on the menu frog legs were being served. It was also quite late, but the restaurant was still open the restaurant owner was happy to have us come in at the late hour. He did not I'm sure expect to see a group of our size, speaking English too, enter at that time of the evening.

It just happened that one of the people working at the restaurant was taking English lessons. So that employee was very happy to have people to practice his English with we all had a good time. I had a very good time and my first time of ever eating frog meat. When everyone's menu was ordered, Haruko at my request and for me, ordered frog. Everyone's food was delivered, I think my food came last, maybe because the frog had to be prepared. When it was ordered, most of the group wanted to taste a little frog meat because of having never dined on frog meat. I know I never had, so I promised the group they could have a taste of my frog when it came. When my food arrived, the frog was on a separate dish all cooked very nice and stretched on a dish, less the head. Resembling a person in a way, perhaps if it had been cut in pieces, it would have been different. I remember members of the group took a small piece to taste the frog and no more Haruko did too also said she used to kill frogs with stones when she was small, living in Yamanashi-ken, but did not care for frog legs much on that night.

That was okay, I enjoyed it the frog tasted like chicken to me. The legs were especially good, haven't eaten any frog meat since that time in Kyoto or anywhere since that time either, I guess frogs have their way. We all went camping one time in Bakersfield with my son Henry at a place called Balch Park a fair-sized camping ground, near a little river, I can remember a bear came around the little river looking for fish parts people left when cleaning their fish. The first night we were there, my son had a dog he left the dog outside the first night but let the dog sleep in the little folding tent trailer he borrowed from his friend the next night, the dog was happy. I guess the dog didn't like spending the night with the bears roaming around. There were also lots of large green bullfrogs at the park. Each night we were there, the moon seemed close, big, full, round, and had a yellow most beautiful color, also, was very bright. The frogs croaked and sang their frog songs day and night, it seemed they sang more loudly at night. Maybe cricket's too joined the frogs choir at night. Their choir created a nice feeling as we sat around the campfire roasting hot dogs, eating rice balls, corn, potatoes, drinking hot tea and cold drinks. We all had a very nice time at Balch Park.

Must have, it's still remembered and that has been close to 20 years maybe or more, ago. During the visit to Japan I mentioned before, we also visited Yokohama, Tokyo and Haruko's birthplace in Yama-nashi-Ken, Japan. We did much traveling on that trip, it was a nice visit and a nice trip. Haruko always enjoyed having the children and their families come for visits and bring their grandchildren. Especially on the holidays, she would prepare so many of her Japanese dishes, the children enjoyed them and she loved making them. For Thanksgiving, Christmas, and New Year especially it seemed the mochi. She bought a little mochi machine, she would carefully mix the batter the machine I think, would cook the batter, I know when the batter was just right it would twist, turn, and do everything with the batter. When the batter was correct Haruko would remove it from the machine, place it on a table. It would be steaming hot when removed from the machine, after it was made flat from rolling with a roller on the table. Haruko would let it cool and then cut it up in about 2 inch squares for making her special dishes for family and friends to enjoy all except me her husband. Haruko knew this, she always took my mochi out and let it dry. She would later break it up into little pieces and fry it, she knew I liked it that way. Seems a lot of other folks including my wife did too, I know it disappeared fast, mochi seems to do that. When Haruko and I were in Japan years ago, maybe fifty or sixty years ago, mochi was made by men swinging big wooden mauls, and was a pretty big operation. Now lots of people have those little machines. Haruko usually made mochi for the holidays, usually New Years.

One little store in Salinas California, where we settled after retirement from the Army, had most items Haruko needed for cooking dishes she enjoyed from her country. So when she desired to prepare for the children's visit, or her friends visits, she had no trouble finding ingredients of most any type she needed. As I have said before, Haruko was an excellent cook. she could barbecue turkeys, steaks, fish, anything on the barbecue grill. When her brother's, or relation came from Japan, they always took pictures and enjoyed Haruko's big golden brown BBQ turkeys from the barbecue grill. Turkeys are probably pretty safe in Japan, but in America they have to watch out especially around Thanksgiving, Christmas, or New Year's because they just might be barbecued, maybe pretty soon in Japan too. I think Haruko and I seen barbecue grills in the markets over there too. Haruko usually had a little garden at most of the places we stayed. I know when we were stationed in Redstone Arsenal in Alabama, she had a little garden, a pretty good-sized little garden because in our little housing area, each family if they wanted to, could plant a little garden. We were there for almost 6 years, Haruko and I would put in a little garden.

I was always amazed how she would want a little wood type frame prepared for most of her long Japanese cucumbers. They would climb over this wood frame and hang down. Guess that's the way she was used to doing things cucumber wise in her country. I soon learned, fixed the little wood frame for her, got out of the way and helped Haruko raise her cucumbers and other little garden things. Haruko also liked to go with her friends on bus trips to Las Vegas and Reno, sometime they would go for a 3 or 4 day trip. At times they would make a few dollars and Haruko would come back so happy, she really liked any little amount won on the one armed Bandit machines over there. Which was not won often, but the ladies had a lot of fun and that's what they went there for.

Retirement life was much different for Haruko, the family, and I. No more military life. No more Okinawa, or traveling to different military bases. Wherever they might be, life was really different. I had been in the Army for 25 years, it was quite a transition, quite a change. Haruko handled the change very well, she adapted to civilian life pretty well, myself I think I did, It was a big change for me. No more military duties, no more working with the troops coming home from that, or anything like that

Our Sons

Albert and William on their wedding day. Both married at the same place and on the same day. We got 2 daughters in law at the same place, same day, and same time.

The Magnet

I could climb mountains
I could soar stars
I could walk deserts
I could go far
I could swim rivers
Go over waterfalls too
There isn't much I wouldn't go thru
But I can't, you're not there
You're the magnet that
Pulls, like a strong golden hair
A light through the dark that beams-
And you're there, and it isn't strange
Quite like a rainbow too
You've always been there
You've helped pull me thru
So now the mountains to climb
The stars, rivers too
I still can do.
If you and my memories
Will stroll with me, thru.

Everything was all civilian now and being a civilian after having been military 25 years is a big change, It affects all people differently. Haruko was very understanding she was sure we discussed and understood most any problem together in the very positive manner. We had always followed in our marriage all the way through our marriage, to try and solve a problem before sundown. Because if it carries over till the next day it usually is twice as bad with more vengeance. Haruko was always there with very good communication and excellent understanding. That really helps in a marriage to have communication. I know it really helped when I retired from the Army after my 25 years of active duty and the return to civilian life of which I really had never really experienced. Because I finished high school at the age of 17 years of age and entered the Army. Don't get me wrong it was a good life, the military was good to me, I enjoyed the military life and still do at 86 years of age. Those memories are great, of course there were always good, bad times, but that's to be expected, that's life. Haruko's understanding really helped very much when we moved to being complete civilians in a very big way, it was quite a shock. We had to do most things different, I was then 42 years old, not very old, but most civilian residents of 42 year's age had been at their occupations for many year's.

Possible

In Winter I believe
Summer will come.
When lost I believe
There is still a way
If you till, plant seeds, and water
The ground I believe
A seed will grow.
I believe that after storms
A rainbow will come
And light the sky
And birds will fly.
I believe a small candle lit
Placed in the dark
Will light the dark with
Silent love.
I believe love brings lovely.
I believe faith brings
Lasting wonders.
I believe love and faith
Is wondrous, spiritual
And eternal
In winter I believe
Summer will come
In the dark I believe
The sun will shine.
I believe thru belief
And love and faith.
The impossible
That is possible....
Is possible.

Honors

An honorable
Occupation
Whatever it may be
Gives occasion and a reason
Whatever
The season-
To beautiful
Honors be.
In lovely
Ways.

Our daughter Kuniko Marie
graduating from high school.

But with patience and our family understanding we would always talk this over where Haruko seemed to understand and suggest to use patience, keep trying to work things out. Using those methods with Haruko and the family, neighbors, friends, and of course with my own cooperation the change to civilian life was pretty quick. The children didn't have much trouble because my daughter was already gone and graduated from high school. She had been working with the telephone company for quite a few years was married and had her own family. I believe. soon or very soon after retirement had our first grandchild. So our daughter was no problem, in fact she and her husband were very helpful in helping Haruko and I make the change to civilian life. My boys were quite large too, our oldest son graduated from high school in Okinawa a few days before we left Okinawa to come back to retire. I came back from Okinawa to Fort Ord California and about a week later I was retired, and was a civilian. Haruko the family and I took a deep breath and off we were to the big change in life. We, on looking back, took it in stride and I must credit my very understanding and very helpful wife and family for their cooperation and understanding at the time for we had much to do, at that time, to suddenly do. How to find work, get a home, which was quite easy, there was a big building boom going on. We got a home in Salinas where we have been since 1972, when I retired from the Army. Haruko liked it here of course we all liked it here in Salinas, the weather is nice, not too hot and not too cold, just moderately nice.

When I retired, my older son went on to college, he attended a junior college in Monterey California for a while, and finished at UCLA in Los Angeles California. Our younger son finished high school in Salinas and went on to college. Then went to Japan for a few years studied martial arts, got a 3rd degree black belt in martial arts and worked in corrections facilities for many years. Our older son had his own business for many years, Haruko and I enjoyed and really enjoy the family retirement years. Little bits and pieces. little sprinkles of life together I've mentioned and some more I must speak of now that I think of them as I write of them while I'm camping in my old van today. Also thinking back through the days, weeks, years, and back now, as they pass under the wide open skies. Of Haruko, next month will be 6 years since the Creator called for her on April 15th 2010, six years ago at our home in Salinas California at about 11:30 that evening she was called by the Creator. All must answer when the Creator calls. I remember the old times, way back at her friend's little laundry, the little laundry where we GI's got our laundry done in Yokohama, Japan.

Your Day

With sunshine
To brighten and enlighten
Your day
A Touch of blue sky
Along the way
A wish, a hope
And who can say
What one can accomplish
On such a day.

Korea 1950-1951

I came one day, Haruko was there talking with a friend whose parents owned the laundry. Her friend told me, this is my friend Haruko, she's a nice person."

She introduced Haruko we met and became friends, made a friendship that lasted for years, from about February of 1948. Remembering from the start at that little laundry, courtship through the following months my return to America. Going back to the far east, thorough the Korean War, a hospital stay at 8th station hospital in Kobe Japan, of Haruko coming there, my working at the hospital for a while, getting our marriage papers started, My return to Korea from the hospital and while there getting, finishing the paperwork. Then getting married on rest leave from Korea. Returning to Korea and finishing my time there. Picking up Haruko in Japan and starting our family life in America, the Creator helped us all the way through. I've spoken of this before in the story, but will try to recall more incidents of our lives as they happened. If I can recall maybe not all but some as they happened through the years of quite a few. When Haruko and I got to America, we got off the ship in Seattle. The troop ship I think it was the M. M. Patrick, anyway we got off the ship and went by bus to my new station in Fort Ord California where I remained for about two years working.

You

I found you my wife
In a country far away
And brought you
To my country one fine day.
And happy we have been
Here far away.
We found our home
Raised a family, have grandchildren
Great grandchildren too.
The days have grown long…
And years so have they.
Tho in it all… No matter what
Each day or year
I brought you here
And here we'll always be
In this country now both ours…
Growing old, more lovely
Everyday.

Lincoln Avenue Church
Salinas, CA

There as an automotive school instructor we got government quarters Haruko got her first taste of American housing there. We got some converted G I barracks to government quarters, that were quite comfortable. Haruko got to use an American cook stove with an oven, in Japan she had used a hibachi, a little charcoal burning cooking device. She caught on to using the cook stove, with other American cooking devices very quickly. Also we got an old automobile the Army loaned us some housing items for our living quarters and we purchased some. Haruko got to do shopping in American stores quite soon after her arrival in the Monterey area. Also she found other Japanese brides there. The service men returning with, that were married in the Far East, Japan, Korea, other places. Also the ladies found stores where they could find food they were familiar with, and stores where they could shop, and speak their language. I believe in the Autumn of the same year, Haruko came to America we went by Greyhound bus to Michigan from California to visit my family, Haurko got to meet my family, they were very fond of her, she also was fond of them. This friendship has continued through the years. After about two years at Ft. Ord. California, I was sent to Ladd Air Force Base in Alaska, to a little medical unit there, at Fairbanks, Alaska, served as the unit's motor Sgt.

I drove my old Dodge car to Seattle Washington and sent it to Alaska when Haruko came, met her at the train depot in Fairbanks Alaska with my old car. We then started our life in Alaska, in a little house I had rented off-base till we got quarters on base. Haruko got to have lots of salmon fish which at this time I assume is still quite plentiful there. The time now in 2016 that was about 1953 and 1954, quite a few years have passed. We also there got quite a few moose steaks, caribou meat, and snowshoe rabbit meat which Haruko would not eat. She did not care for a wild animal meat, but she kind of liked Alaska, it was cold in winter, sometime in winter I saw the thermometer drop to 63 degrees below zero, that's quite cold. Very cold, of course the military was prepared for the extreme weather conditions, our Government Quarters were very comfortable, in the summer though Fairbanks would get to 92 degrees above. Farmers there raised a very large items like cabbage because the growing season is so short. June 21st I think is the year's longest day, summers there have long hours of sunlight, winters short hours. Alaska is quite a place, of course then, it then was a territory, now it's a state. Our oldest son was born in Alaska and is now over 60 years of age time passes or time is, and we pass, something like that. Our youngest son was born in Madigan General Hospital in Tacoma Washington. Haruko acquired her American citizenship in Alaska she and I studied really hard together for the test. She passed it with flying colors and was quite happy. Having been in the military and in the military for many years after marriage, Haruko and

I traveled many places in the military as I've already mentioned traveled practically all over the United States, she I and the children.

Haruko drove our many automobiles for many years, she learned to drive on a huge Ford Thunderbird automobile we had. I think it was a 1956 Ford Thunderbird, a nice automobile. Then she drove many cars we acquired after that drove all the many bases and places we traveled to. But one day when I came home she said I don't want to drive anymore, I asked her why and she said I just don't want to drive anymore and she never did, she never did say why. I'll never forget our many experiences of raising our children from their birth through childhood, puberty, teenage years, to be out on their own. They were interesting years and we did them together. Seen all our children get married, give us grandchildren, great-grandchildren, great, great, grandchildren. One of my hobbies is camping, Haruko wasn't too fond of camping, but she always went along, we performed some of the many methods of camping from tent, VW camper, got an old motor home too, still have a camper I use quite often. Haruko always went along, I think she had fun too. We always took the children, when they married and had their families. They and their families would also come along, we would go to KOA Campgrounds, rent cabins and with our various type camping equipment we had fun, years of enjoyment.

Haruko and Charlie at Ladd
Air Force Base Housing area
Fairbanks, Alaska 1954

The Ship

One evening the ship, with one
I loved
Sailed quietly
Not at Full Sail
But away.
To where the ocean
And the sky meet as one
The ship, the ship
With one
I loved a board
Then disappeared from view
For me- to see
I, at that time, said to me
My love, my love
Is gone, forever
Gone from me.
Perhaps others far away
If the ship with my love
Sails in at full sail someday.
May say, here she comes, here she comes
This I'll never know.
I only know one evening
The ship with my love
Sailed quietly away.

Also around the home, and in various experiences through the years I can never forget Haruko and I growing with the children, grandchildren also through birthdays, Thanksgivings, thorough Christmas, New Years. Those memorable experiences family together experiences, never-to-be-forgotten experiences, lifelong experiences we have experienced together, they were beautiful. They still are, give, just give, and always will give memories. Haruko someway, her way, I think and at times I feel spiritually to be here in her way. Thorough favorite pictures of her, thorough memories. As I've said before in this writing, Haruko was a lovely wonderful person and a wife for me and to be, it seemed in her country, waiting for me from my country to find, and we to marry, and enjoy our years, our Creator given happy years, with our families together. It certainly seemed that way. I will always believe the Creator arranged it that way. Thorough faith and faith is powerful, for to believe, with faith much can be accomplished, and I believe Haruko and I had much faith and belief and love, in and for each other.

Comprehend

It's hard for we to comprehend
The rays of rising sun
Or things it's rays
Just mean to us
Each one by chosen one
It's hard for we to comprehend
Each noon time, twilight evening too
Or seconds, minutes, hours
Days or years, as we
That through them stray.
But as the sun that gives us light
Also stars that twinkle- oh so bright
The moon was shimmering
Silvery light.
The creations Creator with
Eternal guiding light
Guides us spiritually
In all we ask, seek, and do
And comprehends, rewards
As warm rays of rising sun
With guiding love to us
Faithfully all the way everyday.
Tho it's hard for we to comprehend
We pray for you
And your family and-
Prayers power, has… no end.

Of Love

Mountains are difficult
Hard to climb
But at the top there's brilliant
Bright sunshine
Clouds on the way hard to see through
Help mountains appear anywhere too.
But if there's a will
To climb to the top
To see through the fog
To see through the dark
To dream of the day
To dream of a way
Where sunshine of day
Will light a pathway
To head on ward and thru
And change the way
That love can flow.
Then mountains can be paths of healing eternal
Love…
To Heaven High.

Okinawa

Love… now love, is like the sunshine above. It shines in its way through nights and days, guides in its way silently. To goal's untold that produces only the beautiful, along with faith and belief. Thorough our marriage Haruko and I, … I believe, that we reached our goal, a goal given by the Creator through faith and belief. From our meeting, in the countries thousands of miles apart, thorough our marriage, the raising of our families, our years together, our faith, belief in each other, our love for each other. Though the Creator called for Haruko. Our love spiritually remains, always will, for always, always. For true, faith, belief, love, including the Creator's is, was, and always is forever. I feel and believe that way… With the lovely and with love, I do.

The Twenty-Third Psalm

The Lord is my shepherd; I shall not want.

He maketh me to lie down in green pastures: he leadeth me beside the still waters.

He restoreth my soul: he leadeth me in the paths of righteousness for his name's sake.

Yea, though I walk through the valley of the shadow of death, I will fear no evil: for thou art with me; thy rod and thy staff they comfort me.

Thou preparest a table before me in the presence of mine enemies: thou anointest my head with oil; my cup runneth over.

Surely goodness and mercy shall follow me all the days of my life: and I will dwell in the house of the Lord forever.

Lincoln Avenue Presbyterian
Church in Salinas, CA

There's A Reason

Arr. by GIANNI STAIANO

Slow Gospel swing

AL VICENT

There's a

rea - son for the sun - shine in the sky   There's a
rea - son that God sends his love each day   To each

rea - son why the birds fly by on high   For this is
one in his own ve - ry spe - cial way   For this is

love in Na - ture's way for love al - ways finds a way There's a
love from God a - bove and God's love it finds a way

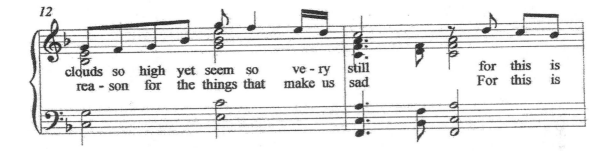

In Loving Memory of Haruko Vicent.
September 15th, 1921- April 15th, 2010

Met

We met in the land of near far away
And love grew by days and years in a way
That lasted and was true like skies, that are blue
With rainbows that glow of beautiful
After storms pass through
But storms must come for all to see
Then storms will pass
And we with love, will better see
This through the years
We together learned to do
Much together we learned
Raised our family, and with
Others, the Creator's love, made it thru
Thru with lovely memories of love
From when we met, Haruko and I
In the land of Japan, near far away
And have grown together by days and years
In loves way.

Your Husband

Albert E. Vicent

My Special Place

When I was young a special place that I liked to be was to walk on the railroad tracks that was easy to do because we lived in a very small town after the train had went by it was several hours before another would arrive and we knew their schedules, so we walked on the track it was safe and easy to do and also there were miles and miles of railroad track and open space to walk letting one's imagination wildly soar as desired.

On occasion I could see a deer with its young sometime close and sometime distant, in the trees near the tracks, also many wild berries in the summer. Blue berries, strawberries, June berries and blackberries That grew nicely along the tracks because the old steam engines would blow off steam as they went along the tracks which was like rain to the plants and they grew quite well there. The rail beds were cleaned which help plants to grow and my brother, friends and I walked for hours sometimes eating, gathering berries, eating them and pretending.

In my special place I could feel the warmth of the sun's rays in the summer, the coolness of the autumn, the cool snow in winter as the seasons penetrated one's skin. Also raindrops as they fell light sometimes heavy from the sky. Lightning and thunder in the summer could be felt sometimes scary, but nice in a way because when it was finished the sun would come out and we could usually see rainbows and rainbows are always beautiful and nice, you can almost feel them. They seem close by, but really aren't.

Sometimes I could hear a whippoorwill calling near the evening hours. It's permeating lovely it makes you stop and listen, especially when you're alone. Because it's lonesome, lovely, beautiful, and kind of spiritual in a way and it seems that even leaves on the trees listen with you. Then there's the Nighthawk that could be heard in my special place. With its swooping diving call, and the rustle of trees, a cowbell because some people had cows that roamed freely throughout the country area then.

The smell there was fresh and clean, the smell of country air with nothing but trees and fresh air from nearby hills with wildflowers. A passing train with its coal smoke and a few flying cinders, mixed with fresh country air. Of course smoke from chimneys of houses and home cooking could be smelled at times too.

Sometimes in my special place I would take a corn bread and salt bacon and butter sandwich, along with a peanut butter and jelly sandwich. Then disappear, to where the strawberries, plums, wild plums, blueberries were, in the summer, and in the winter, to where the winter, and I were. Also, I remember opening my mouth and tasting snowflakes when they are falling, they're delicious, mixed with the country taste of fresh air.

The light there was always bright from the sun, from childhood, from kerosene lamps. There was no electric power in the town but everything was warmly lit, lovely I think because I don't remember dark nights. I can feel the mosquito bites, the cold from the snow in the winter and damp falling rain but the feeling is nice. Like the touch of warm sunshine on my head that seems to warm all over, like warm water in a bathtub, it feels good

In my special place I would run thorough the grass chasing butterflies, pretending I was a cowboy. Sometimes a sailor on a pirate ship and it was fun, great fun. But I always wanted to drive a train. I remember one time one of the engineers let my brother and I climb up on an engine of one of the steam locomotives used back then. He showed us the many gauges, where the whistle was, how to ring the bell and a lot of things. I'll always remember that, it was great.

I always wanted to drive a ship, a submarine and a motorcycle with a sidecar, and I did in my imagination from my special place. An overwhelming feel, I had from my special place was to travel to places, of the far, far away. I used to travel on an imaginary flying carpet in my walks, sometimes from my special place, to places like China where I would dine with people there, to Egypt and ride camels, to Spain and listen to guitars, and then return to my special place feeling really good. From history books I could read of these places, in my imagination I could travel there for no one could stop me, in my special place.

The old steam trains don't run there anymore but the railroad bed is still there in Michigan. I plan to visit there this summer and see if my magic blanket and Imagination can still operate because it's really lovely to have a special private place to see, hear, feel, smell, touch, move and think things in your own private special place where you can be, that special you.

Bye

Maybe my special place was preparing me for the future years when I would meet the lady I was to marry, Haruko. She also, lived in a country area, but in Japan, across the ocean far away. In a country area which was much the same as my country area only, she lived in her country a few years more early, because she was a few years older than I. But our experiences at the time in our lives of living in the country area may have been somewhat the same. Often times during our many years of marriage, Haruko and I used to talk over our younger years of life. Much of the things like bird, animal sounds, insects, lightning, thunder and naturally the seasons all except the snow, because in Haruko's country where she lived it did not snow. Otherwise except for the difference in our culture, the way we do things. To accomplish what we want of our desires was much the same.

Of course what I have written in this book previously about my wife and I, is much the same, but I wanted to include some of the same, but not really the same because it comes with a little about country in it. My special place in the country in Michigan where my childhood years were spent, I've never forgotten, and when Haruko first went with me to visit my family all but my father, for he passed away my senior year in high school. When I took Haruko to visit with my family after bringing her to America I pointed out to her most of the area of my special childhood place to her. Also how some of the imaginary places I would travel to like China, Japan, other places. After High School that I actually did travel to Japan, met her and came back to America, went back, through part of the Korean War, married her and we raised our family, we talked about it many times. When we would visit Michigan to visit my family we always would go to my special place in Peacock Michigan, these times are quite sentimental in their own special ways and are quite unforgettable to me. I have kind of attached a lot of my childhood dreams to have later sprouted to reality from, perhaps having been silently, quietly, maybe imagined from there.

Anyway Haruko and I many times visited my special place, and we were together, lovingly together, married for 58 and one half years. We met each other February1948 altogether about 61 years, when the Creator called her on April 15th 2010. We spent many beautiful, sentimental, unforgettable, lovely years together. I will never forget her.

An Experience

To pray is a beautiful experience
Lovely as the dawn
Sunlight, moon, stars at night
It enlightens as vastness
Of waters on the Earth
Prayer gives oneness like
Birds that soar in the skies
Of blue near the heavens- of love
To pray yields a closeness
With the Creator of all
That patiently waits for our call
And provides help to our words
Many or few.
With the Holy Spirit giving always
Giving a new, meaning- that
Praying is a most…
Beautiful experience.

Haruko the writing
Of this book came
Quick and slow too
An experience
Kind of like
A prayer
From the Creator
And in a way
As if the heavens
Opened
With only the lovely
Through memory
About you,
Haruko and I.
It was
A most
Beautiful experience
An experience
Kind of like- a prayer
From the Creator
And,
Thank you Haruko
For those many
Eternally beautiful
Years we had together
They will forever
And ever
Be remembered
As the forever
Of seasons,
With love.

Your Husband.

Printed in the United States
By Bookmasters